ADAM WALBURG

SMOKING SOLUTIONS

The Ultimate Guide on How to Stop Smoking, Discover Effective Tips on How to Break Your Smoking Habit and Revitalize Your Body

Descrierea CIP a Bibliotecii Naţionale a României
ADAM WALBURG
   SMOKING SOLUTIONS. The Ultimate Guide on How to
Stop Smoking, Discover Effective Tips on How to Break Your
Smoking Habit and Revitalize Your Body / Adam Walburg –
Bucharest: Editura My Ebook, 2021
   ISBN

ADAM WALBURG

SMOKING SOLUTIONS

**The Ultimate Guide on How to Stop Smoking,
Discover Effective Tips on How to Break Your
Smoking Habit and Revitalize Your Body**

My Ebook Publishing House
Bucharest, 2021

TABLE OF CONTENTS

INTRODUCTION

Being an arguably difficult addiction to overcome, the individual would need to have all the necessary tools available to help in the quest to overcome this addiction successfully and permanently. Get all the info you need here.

CHAPTER 1

BEATING NICOTINE BASICS

Synopsis

Being an arguably difficult addiction to overcome, the individual would need to have all the necessary tools available to help in the quest to overcome this addiction successfully and permanently.

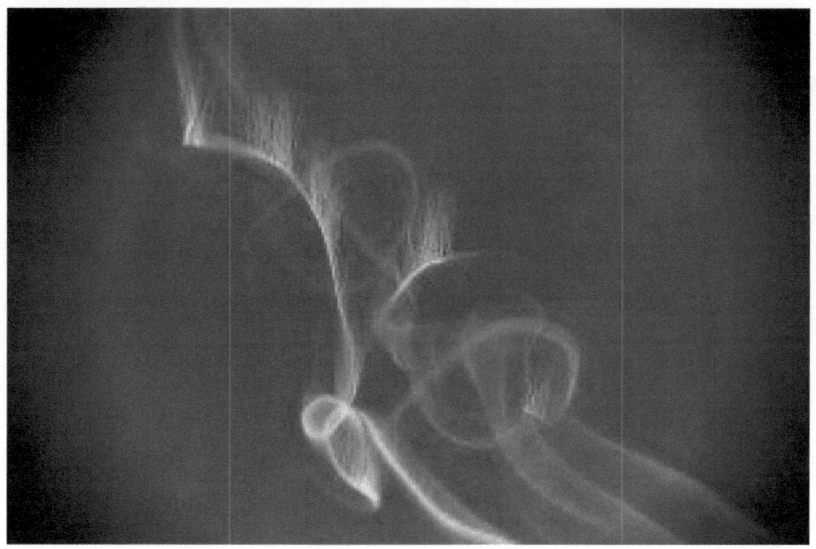

The Basics

One should understand the connection between the brain and the body and the way it clings on to the addiction as it will help to further strengthen the resolve to beat the addiction. It is without a doubt, that a person will not be able to quit smoking overnight, but there are some ways to either try cutting down with the eventual goal of quitting in mind or to simply choose options that are the lesser of two evils.

Some experts would recommend starting with switching to non commercial brand cigarettes as these do not contain additives that the regular commercial ones are touted to contain. These chemicals could run into combinations of as much as 4000 different chemicals.

Another element to be aware of when it comes to the habit of smoking would be the reason it has become rather habitual. Looking into the trigger point that causes the individual to seek out a cigarette may eventually help the individual to control the situation and eliminate the trigger point which will eventually decrease the need to turn to a cigarette for relief.

Peer pressure could also be a very significant contributor to the idea of smoking, in turn making it rather hard to beat. Making the effort to consciously avoid situations where smoking is acceptable and even expected would be a good start.

CHAPTER 2

NICOTINE REPLACEMENTS

Synopsis

There are several different ways that can be tried in the quest to stop smoking and in turn stop the nicotine dependency. These would include several different ways that one should explore where there is a platform that allow the individual to seek suitable replacements for the nicotine habit.

Substitutes

The following are some tried and true methods that are often recommended for nicotine replacement exercises:

Nicotine gum – this is a type of over the counter remedy that is the most popular choice for first time attempts to beat the nicotine dependency.

It is usually available at any local pharmacy and does not need a doctor's prescription. The gum when chewed, will allow the nicotine to be absorbed into the body without the individual having to resort to the act of smoking.

However this method should only be used for a period of not more than six months.

Nicotine patch – is another time of medication that can be applied to the skin each day with the intention of curbing the need to light up a cigarette for the nicotine fix.

The milder brands do not require a doctor's prescription while the more potent one would certainly require some medical recommendation and sometimes even intervention.

Bupropion hydrochloride – these are pills that do not actually contain any nicotine but are used to combat the nicotine cravings.

It is usually used with the direction of a medical professional who in turn monitors the progress of the individual choosing this method of nicotine replacement.

Using NRT is also another option to explore in the quest to find a suitable nicotine replacement. The nicotine medication contains such negligible amounts of the negative substance that it very rarely eventually becomes an addiction thus effectively allowing the individual another alternative until the nicotine craving is no longer evident.

CHAPTER 3

USING SELF HYPNOSIS

Synopsis

Some people have successfully chosen to use self hypnosis as a way to overcome the nicotine addiction. However it should be noted that nicotine replacement therapy does not necessarily work for everyone but it does have a rather impressive track record. Self hypnosis is widely recognized as an effective way of helping addicts to stop smoking.

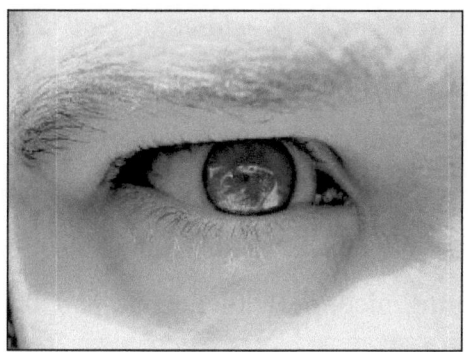

Using Hypnosis

The action of self hypnosis is actually the act of allowing the mind to focus on the activity of smoking. The mind will go into a state where the hypnotic platform established will be influenced by the incoming stimuli which is kept consistent.

The mind will have to readjust the current thought process that accepts smoking as normal and a seemingly uneventful and natural act, to another mindset that encourages the thought of revulsion and total disinterest in such as activity.

The hypnotic influence the self hypnosis would have to create would be that there is no longer a need to be influenced and directed to smoke every time the urge to do so takes over the person's thought process.

The daily elements the mind is "fed" with in terms of the acceptability of the smoking addiction can be expanded and contracted within the boundaries of the mind until they change the thought process either for better or worse.

Thus there is every possibility of creating a positive influence which will extend to the mind rejecting the need to smoke or have the nicotine addiction as part of the daily life cycle of the individual.

There are a lot of self hypnosis methods and books available for the individual to explore but the main idea would be to ensure the hypnosis is to be the focus of firmly changing the behavior into a more positive one.

CHAPTER 4

USING SUPPORT GROUPS

Synopsis

Although smoking is considered basically an individual act, trying to stop the habit would almost always require the help of outside influences and participation. One of the more productive ways of getting the individual on the right track to quitting this negative habit would be to get the support of a group focused on the same agendas.

Using Groups

There are many support groups that are formed to help those in need of such group reinforcement to kick the smoking habit. These groups are usually experienced in handling all the various aspects that the individual would eventually encounter through the process of trying to kick the habit.

The support given could range anywhere from simple being there to listen to helping the individual through the craving and severe withdrawal symptoms when attacked.

Most people find that the support given is very helpful as it comes from people who have been through the same experience and have come out of it successfully.

This is certainly better than having to listen to people who have never been through the same challenge, thus are not really able to relate to the situation in a primal manner.

The members of the group are usually more than willing to reach out to each other and provide the much needed support at the time it is most desperately needed.

The platform facilitated to be able to talk about the problem openly without the pressure of having to endure unnecessary criticism and accusations, allows those seeking conform and strength to kick the habit to find it here.

Being able to talk about the struggles and very real feelings is a very powerful tool to help get the individual through the initial stages of attempting to kick the habit. The information extended within the group sessions can also be rather invaluable to the participants.

CHAPTER 5

USING NUTRITION

Synopsis

A lot of nutritionists believe that with it is possible to use a balanced and complete diet plan to help combat the need for the body to seek what it lack in the form or smoking or nicotine addiction.

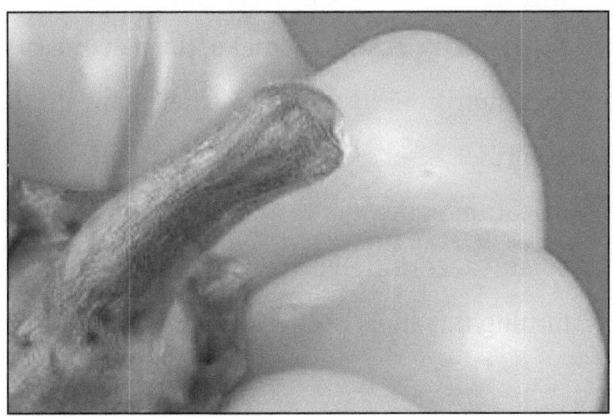

Food

The general perception would be that if the body is satisfied with all the proper vitamins, minerals and nutrients, then the craving for other outside negative elements such as nicotine would not be needed to complete the individual both mentally and physically.

Adequate nutritional intake will help to minimize depression and other negative feelings such as being anxious, tired, over excited and any other abnormal behavioral patterns, thus adequately eliminating the need for the individual to turn to smoking as a quick fix, when things are not going smoothly.

In some cases the nicotine will further enhance these negative feelings rather than help to minimize them.

When a person is ready to make the necessary changes towards a better nutritionally balanced diet plan, the body and mind will be further strengthened and this will allow for the natural detoxification pathways to allow all the toxins within the body to dissipate accordingly, thus the individual would be weary of disturbing this ideal scenario with the smoking habit.

Having a healthy diet plan in place will also help the body to work towards detoxifying the body and eliminating all the negative buildups within body due to the smoking habit.

Using nutrition as a combat tool for smoking is also possible, as the healthy body conditions will keep the individual strong and alert thus facilitating the mental and physical machinery to ensure adequate will power is in place to help the individual quit the smoking habit in a consistent and healthy way. A low carb diet is usually recommended as the best choice for helping the individual beat the nicotine habit.

CHAPTER 6

BASICS TO BREAKING OLD HABITS

Synopsis

Change is all about results. If you remain off cigarettes and you're living a satisfying life then that's good. You've exposed your calling and whatever plan (or lack thereof) that you're working appears to be the right fit for you.

In other words, if you're attempting to recover from an addiction, the best thing to do is to do what figures out for you. Instead of taking a hard-line on precisely what needs to be achieved in order to recover, traditional wisdom states you should explore and find what works best.

Where To Start

If someone acquaints you with a program--any plan at all-- you must be realistic about it. Recognize that any plan for change is truly just a collection of suggestions. If a change plan is going to work for you, do you think it's the actual suggestions of the program that bring about the results, or do you think that the results bank more heavily on your personal actions? Just how complicated is a plan of change, truly? It's not what you do; it's how you achieve it. Consider what a great change plan truly consists of. We might break it down like this:

1) Abstinence
2) A blueprint for living
3) Support and networking (assisting others)
4) Personal maturation

Really, where is the mystery in this? Certainly, it's a lot of stuff. And no, it's not unavoidably simple to achieve. Individuals fail at change again and again. But my point is that there's no grand mystery in the plan itself. The answers are in the action.

There's a shift that occurs once the struggling addict in early on change is no more battling to remain free of nicotine; they discover a particular peace about themselves and things start clicking for them. Either that or they relapse. However the idea of transition is real.

Change is split into short-term and long-run change. We do particular things to begin with to remain clean. If we don't alter our strategy eventually and make the transition to long-run change, we relapse. We must change in order to make it over the long run.

We must achieve particular things in early on change to remain clean. These are different things for everyone, but the precepts are the same: we require a strong support system, much structure; some require protection from the outside world (like a treatment center). Still these things won't keep you clean 5 years down the road or even one year out. Those who don't changeover to long-run, holistic living will inevitably slide back into their old behaviors.

No one consciously knows once they're making this jump from short-term to long-run change. It simply occurs. You're able to retrospect, naturally, and discover how you grew through the stage.

So how may we know what to do? How may we help the changeover? The answer to this is what the originative theory is all about. The answer lies in the 3 primary techniques:

1) Treasuring self
2) Networking with others
3) Push for holistic maturation

Particularly, the push for holistic maturation is a critical component of the transition. I'm not so certain that you're able to plan this sort of growth out specifically, however. What's
26

crucial is to get past the mentality of "I'm just going to focus on my plan and not get distracted with schooling or career or additional things right now." Many traditional plans don't encourage holistic maturation so if you focus on them then you're going to be doing so at the exclusion of additional growth opportunities.

All the same maturation involves change. We either move onward in change or we slide back.

So my proposal is to seek holistic growth opportunities right from the beginning. Find ways to diversify and grow or learn outside of the limits of "traditional change." This may include things like physical fitness, nutrition, meditation, training, the arts, learning new skills, building new relationships, etcetera.

The transition occurs once you grow beyond the minute focus of your early change efforts. Once we're working a traditional plan of change, we tend to have a restricted view in that we perceive all potential growth as being one-dimensional. Maybe the twelve step model has facilitated this idea as the twelve steps are plainly ordered and are in sequence.

Still in holistic living, maturation may be expansive and non-linear. Regardless what program you're working, most individuals don't grow at a regular pace in change. Many of us careen around for a while to begin with, trying to find our footing and merely get through the cravings and urges of every day. Later on, once we have been making holistic growth attempts, our maturation in change may be explosive.

In other words, at times we have to slog through a tough time in change once we see little results from our attempts. The payoff comes eventually once all of our holistic maturation attempts begin paying off down the road at some point.

The only real enemy in long-run change is complacency. After living nicotine free, we no longer battle with daily urges or even with more elusive threats to change like resentments or self-pity. Rather, the true challenge in long-term change is to continue challenging ourselves to mature.

Center on the 3 primary techniques and continue pushing yourself to grow, and complacency will take care of itself. Once we're first beginning in change, there are a few high impact matters that we may do in order to get going on the right foot. These are action oriented matters we may do, like:

1) Attend treatment
2) Attend meetings
3) Call our sponsor or additional recovering addicts
4) Examine change literature or write up step work

And so forth. These are the sorts of things that are normally suggested to newbies in change. Why? Because they work. They help.

Best is to challenge yourself to mature in your change and develop as a spiritual being. What does this entail? It means that instead of ditching your issues and sniveling in a meeting daily, you ought to be spending your energy in richer ways as you advance in change. One way to achieve this would be to provide addiction help to others.

You may likewise seek to discover new ways to grow outside of the limits of traditional change. For example, the twelve step plan typically centers on spiritual growth solely. This is a shortsighted viewpoint and to really recover you have to heal your life in additional ways too, including physically, emotionally, socially, etc. In order to recover, you have to live this way.

CHAPTER 7

NUTRITIONAL TIPS FOR CONQUERING CIGGY CRAVINGS

Synopsis

Blood sugar plummets in a lot of People when first quitting. The commonest side effects experienced during the first days might frequently be traced back to blood sugar issues. Symptoms like headache, inability to focus, vertigo, time sensing distortions, and the ubiquitous sweet tooth found by many, are frequently affiliated with this blood sugar drop.

Think About The Food

The symptoms of low blood sugar are essentially the same symptoms as not getting enough oxygen, similar to reactions experienced at high altitudes. The reason being the poor supply of sugar and/or oxygen means the brain is getting an incomplete fuel. If you've plenty of one and not plenty of the other, your brain can't operate at any sort of optimal level. Once you quit smoking, oxygen levels are frequently better than they've been in a while, however with a modified supply of sugar it can't properly fuel your brain.

If you use food to raise blood sugar levels, it literally takes up to 20 minutes from the time you chew and swallow the food before it's discharged to the blood, and thus the brain, for its desired effect of fueling your brain. Cigarettes, by carrying out a drug interaction get the body to give up its own stores of sugar, however not in twenty minutes however commonly in a matter of minutes. In a way, your body hasn't had to give up sugar from food in years; you've done it by utilizing nicotine's drug effect!

This is why many People truly gorge themselves on food upon quitting. They start to go through a drop in blood sugar and instinctively get hold of something sweet. Upon finishing the food, they still feel symptoms. Naturally they do, it takes them a moment or two to eat, however the blood sugar isn't hiked up for another 18 minutes. As they're not feeling instantly better, they devour a bit more. They carry on eating increasingly more food, moment after moment till they at last start to feel better.

Again if they're waiting for the blood glucose to go up we're talking of 20 minutes after the 1st swallow. People may eat a lot of food in 20 minutes. However they start to trust that this was the amount required before feeling better. This may be replicated many times throughout the day therefore causing many calories being ingested and inducing weight gain to become a real risk.

Once you abruptly quit smoking, the body is in sort of a state of loss, not willful how to work normally as it hasn't worked normally in such a while. Generally by the 3rd day, however, your body will readjust and relinquish sugar as it's required. Without consuming any more your body will simply work out how to govern blood sugar more efficiently.

You may find however that you do have to change dietary patterns to one that's more regular for you. Regular isn't what it was as a smoker, however more what it was before you took up smoking . A few People go till evening without eating while they're smokers. If they attempt the same process as ex-smokers they'll have side effects of low blood sugar.

It isn't that there's something wrong with them now; they were abnormal previously for all pragmatic purposes. This doesn't mean they should consume more food, however it may mean they have to redistribute the food consumed to a more scattered pattern so they're getting blood sugar doses throughout the day as nature truly had always intended.

To downplay a few of the true low blood sugar effects of the first few days it truly might help to drink juice throughout the day. After the 4th day however, this should no longer be essential as your body should be able to give up sugar stores if your diet is normalized.

If you're having problems that are indicative of blood sugar issues beyond day 3, it wouldn't hurt speaking to your doctor and perchance acquiring some nutritionary counseling.

CHAPTER 8

BENEFITS OF MEDITATION

Synopsis

Decently executed meditative breathing sessions may contribute to the arresting of treating of respiratory sickness. In a few severe cases the aid of a breathing apparatus is paramount in ensuring the person gets the vital air needed to continue functioning. Utilizing meditative breathing techniques it's possible to slowly wean these patients of the breathing machine.

Calming

As the first and commonest steps in meditation sessions call for the practice of breathing, and becoming very aware of the sounds and feelings this breathing makes, the person is able to train the brain to adjust this breathing patters to suit the need at hand.

Like any other muscles in the body, the diaphragm may get "slothful" when not used to its optimal workings, so through meditation the person is encouraged to visualize the actual diaphragm enlarging, and contracting until the desired optimal state is attained.

These deep breathing exercises are only good if the meditation session is done consistently and cautiously. The deep even slow movements of breathing caused by meditation calms the mind and body.

Through meditative breathing methods, the breath in the lung cavity is increased and this helps to increase the oxygen levels in the blood stream, which successively harmonizes the mind and body to combat any respiratory sickness effectively.

Many respiratory diseases obstruct the breathing patterns at assorted stages, due to blockages. Simply breathing harder or faster won't help the congestion. All the same the meditative style of breathing exercises produces better and fuller breaths.

A few illnesses require particular styles of meditative breathing. Asthma is one select example. Although asthma manifests as a physical symptom, a healthy breathing strategy will help the person address the emotional state of mind that bring on such an attack.

Bronchial asthma is a different respiratory sickness that may be helped by meditative breathing exercises. Perhaps not to the extent of curing the disease but surely to help make the patient more comfortable and less stressed.

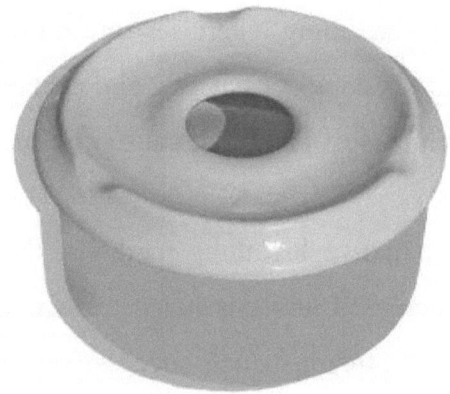

CHAPTER 9

AFFIRMATIONS FOR ABSTINENCE

Synopsis

You are able to utilize affirmations to get yourself thinking and feeling that you do not wish to smoke. All the same, you do not wish to put in references to smoking in your affirmations, merely as you already have a notion that smoking is enjoyable. Once that association has been made in your subconscious mind, any idea of smoking is going to activate a potent desire to smoke.

Rather, you are able to use affirmations to emphasize the benefits of not smoking - without bringing up smoking at all.

Affirming It

Here are a few examples:

- I love being able to breathe freely.

- I love taking exceptional care of my body.

- I nurture my body with sound habits.

- I deserve a clean, fit body.

- I can alter my habits by altering my mind.

- I respect and honor myself always.

- I'm solid enough to defeat any challenge.

- I trust in my might to do anything I wish.

How to use reinforcement

Affirmations work best when they're recited repeatedly and while giving your full focus to them. Not only should you say the words, all the same you ought to likewise do your best to bring forward the corresponding sense associated with the words. For example, if you state, "I feel so strong and empowered" you ought to in reality make an attempt to feel that way. This does take practice if you're not used to controlling your emotional state, all the same it gets easier the more you do it.

Constant repetition a lot of times a day is crucial also, because you're trying to reverse existing beliefs in your subconscious mind.

The illustration affirmations here will assist you in getting you started; all the same feel free to compose your own too!

Affirmations do take time to totally sink in to your subconscious mind, all the same just like your old notions were formed; consistent repetition and reinforcement will assist them in becoming lasting.

CHAPTER 10

HEALTHY HABITS FOR A BETTER LIFE

Synopsis

Do you sweat the small stuff? Do you find strain has increased in your life due to gloomy episodes? Are you searching for a fresh life-style, yet find it hard to relax and find answers?

We have many choices in the world, which gives us the convenience of having fun while choosing a better life-style. When altering your life- style you'll likely have to make decisions that will be hard, yet you are able to do it if you consider yourself and not others.

Remember stress leads to smoking.

Change It

We all have to learn how to relax and take care of ourselves so we may see a brighter future.

We all have to make our life simple. Keeping it simple will help reduce stress. Occasionally we have to give up our homes. The stress of preserving, our home increases. Money commonly becomes a big issue, which causes stress. The care and taxes alone are very stressful for somebody that's living on little money these days.

How to choose:

Do you plan to stay in the same area you live now? Do you want to live in a better climate? The questions demand an answer before mortgaging your home. If you plan to move to a better climate to live healthier, think about the climate.

A lot of us suffer from allergies, hay fever, or other ailments due to climate changes. If you plan to live healthier and reduce, your risks of upper respiratory conditions then consider your options before making a choice to move. You need to consider your budget also. If you're living a fixed-income, consider the low-cost housing projects.

Don't get me wrong there will constantly be some stress in your life that you will not have control of. Now that you've made one of the biggest decision about where you going to live, begin thinking about enjoying life.

Join an exercise group or get a few neighbors to join you for a walk. Walk on sunny days so your body gets natural vitamin D from the sun-rays. The vitamins will help keep your bones strong. Exercising helps keep us fit and is a great way to meet new individuals while having fun.

Don't forget to watch your diet and make certain your getting enough vitamins to keep yourself healthy. If not sure what vitamins you need and how much consult your doctor he may help you make a plan or send you to a dietician to help you with it.

Occasionally we don't eat as much, especially if we have been a smoker so supplement vitamins are needed. Your family health professional can help you with this too.

The world is filled with assorted life-styles, so make your life your own by remaining healthy and avoid sweating the small stuff. Making sound decisions is a great beginning to living free, which promotes health.

CHAPTER 11

THE IMPORTANCE OF QUITTING SMOKING TODAY

Synopsis

There are only benefits when one quits smoking altogether. They are:

Benefits

Financial – Assuming a pack of cigarettes cost $5. Most smokers smoke an average of 10 sticks a day. That means the average smoker needs to have 3.5 packs a week or 14 packs a month.

If one pack costs $5, then the cost of smoking per month is $70. Annually it would cost $840. You can have a pretty good holiday with $840. You can also buy many new things with $840.

You can get an iPad, iPhone, new pc, new golf clubs and many more items. That means you get a bonus of $840 every year for each year that you have given up smoking.

This means going on a holiday or buying a new gadget every year from the money you saved from quitting smoking.

Sociability – Many countries are now enforcing no-smoking zones in public areas like cinemas, shopping malls, government departments, air-con retail outlets, restaurants and others.

Role model – it would be great to quit smoking especially if you have young children. Kids at this age are very impressionable. If they see that their dad or uncle smoke, they would probably be inclined to try it. It would be hypocritical to tell someone not to smoke as it is bad for them when the advice is coming from a smoker.

They will not believe what they hear and will do otherwise. It is recommended to not smoke in front of children. If you need to smoke, do so in a private environment with no fear of affecting anyone.

Wrapping Up

It is becoming very difficult for smokers to operate publicly. There is a stigma regarding smokers and it is catching on with the public. Many smokers are now ostracized from gatherings and invitations. Only close friends and families condone smokers in their presence.

Besides that it is just bad for you. So quit Today!

Daily the ex-smoker should awaken thinking that he isn't going to smoke that day. And every night before he turns in he should to compliment himself for sticking to his goal. As pride is crucial in remaining free from cigarettes.

Not only is it essential, but it's well deserved. For anyone who's quit smoking has broken free from a really powerful addiction. For the first time in a long time, he's gained control over his life, rather than being commanded by his cigarette. For this, he should to be proud.

Printed by Libri Plureos GmbH in Hamburg,
Germany